MY Mood

TRACKER

MY MOOD TRACKER

An Hachette UK Company
www.hachette.co.uk

Summersdale Publishers Ltd
Part of Octopus Publishing Group Limited
Carmelite House
50 Victoria Embankment
LONDON
EC4Y 0DZ
UK

www.summersdale.com

Printed and bound in the Czech Republic

ISBN: 978-1-78783-328-9

Substantial discounts on bulk quantities of Summersdale books are available to corporations, professional associations and other organizations. For details contact general enquiries: telephone: +44 (0) 1243 771107 or email: enquiries@summersdale.com.

MY Mood TRACKER

A JOURNAL TO HELP YOU
MAP YOUR MOOD THROUGH
ALL ITS UPS AND DOWNS

summersdale

Introduction

We all have our off-days - when we're wound up tight, when we're feeling down, or when things just don't feel right. Sometimes we know exactly what's causing the dark cloud... but sometimes the reason isn't so clear.

Enter the mood tracker - a handy tool to help you map your emotions over time. Whether you want to understand how you feel and why, or learn more about your mood patterns, this book has everything you need to see the bigger picture.

As you document your mood every day in the monthly tracker, keep tabs on your sleep, and monitor your diet on the charts in each chapter, a tangible record of you and your mind will begin to emerge. This information not only helps you to navigate your ups and downs but, most importantly, it also helps you to understand more about them.

This journaling method is simple and easy to fit into busy, everyday life. It untangles your feelings and gives you a clear picture of your state of mind - and it puts you firmly in the driving seat. Read on to begin your journey...

You can
do whatever
you put your
mind to

JANUARY

☆- MOOD TRACKER ☆-

Pick a colour or pattern for each category, and colour
in each day's star depending on how you feel.

HOW DO YOU FEEL?

Write down some of the words that describe how you're feeling.

ARE THERE FEELINGS YOU'D LIKE TO CHANGE?

Write down some actions to help you change the way you feel.

Forgive yourself.
We all make mistakes,
but then we make
things worse by beating
ourselves up afterward.
Let go of the guilt.

GLASS half FULL?

Colour in how you felt this month on the glass below.

Fantastic

Great

Good

Average

Down

Bad

Terrible

ENJOY THE LITTLE THINGS

SLEEP TRACKER

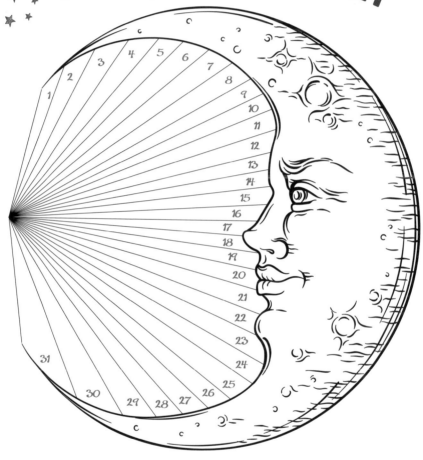

1 2 3 4 5 6 7 8 9 10 11 12 13 14 15 16 17 18 19 20 21 22 23 24 25 26 27 28 29 30 31

☐ Four hours or fewer

☐ Five hours

☐ Six hours

☐ Seven hours

☐ Eight hours

☐ Nine hours or more

BEFORE YOU GO TO SLEEP,
TAKE A LONG HOT SHOWER
OR BATH. FEEL YOUR MUSCLES
RELAX IN THE STEAMY HEAT
AND TAKE SOME TIME ALONE
WITH YOUR THOUGHTS.

FOOD TRACKER

Very healthy

A little unhealthy

Mostly healthy

Very unhealthy

WATER tracker

1 ◊◊◊◊◊	11 ◊◊◊◊◊	21 ◊◊◊◊◊
2 ◊◊◊◊◊	12 ◊◊◊◊◊	22 ◊◊◊◊◊
3 ◊◊◊◊◊	13 ◊◊◊◊◊	23 ◊◊◊◊◊
4 ◊◊◊◊◊	14 ◊◊◊◊◊	24 ◊◊◊◊◊
5 ◊◊◊◊◊	15 ◊◊◊◊◊	25 ◊◊◊◊◊
6 ◊◊◊◊◊	16 ◊◊◊◊◊	26 ◊◊◊◊◊
7 ◊◊◊◊◊	17 ◊◊◊◊◊	27 ◊◊◊◊◊
8 ◊◊◊◊◊	18 ◊◊◊◊◊	28 ◊◊◊◊◊
9 ◊◊◊◊◊	19 ◊◊◊◊◊	29 ◊◊◊◊◊
10 ◊◊◊◊◊	20 ◊◊◊◊◊	30 ◊◊◊◊◊

ONE DROP = 1 GLASS (400 ML)

31 ◊◊◊◊◊

ONE-DAY

Mood tracker

Date: _____

Pick any day of the month and colour in one section per hour
to get a snapshot of your mood over the course of a day.

☆ Great ☆ Good ☆ Average ☆ Poor ☆ Terrible

New Year Playlist

Create a playlist to inspire you throughout the year by jotting down the tunes that make you feel great!

1. _____
2. _____
3. _____
4. _____
5. _____
6. _____
7. _____
8. _____
9. _____
10. _____

Great   Good   Average   Poor   Terrible

HOW DO YOU FEEL?

Write down some of the words that describe how you're feeling.

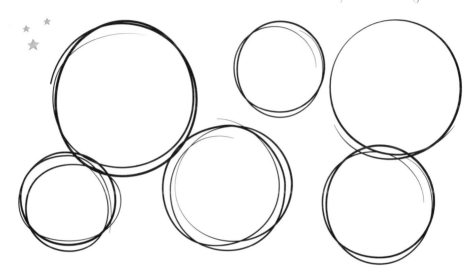

ARE THERE FEELINGS YOU'D LIKE TO CHANGE?

Write down some actions to help you change the way you feel.

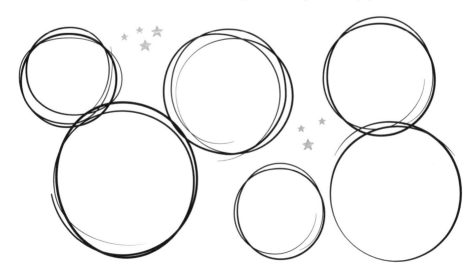

Note to self

If you're finding something difficult, step back. Take a break and focus on something completely different, then come back to it when you are refreshed and ready to try again.

GLASS half FULL ?

Colour in how you felt this month on the glass below.

Fantastic

Great

Good

Average

Down

Bad

Terrible

Nothing is
impossible

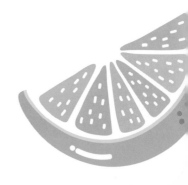

SLEEP TRACKER

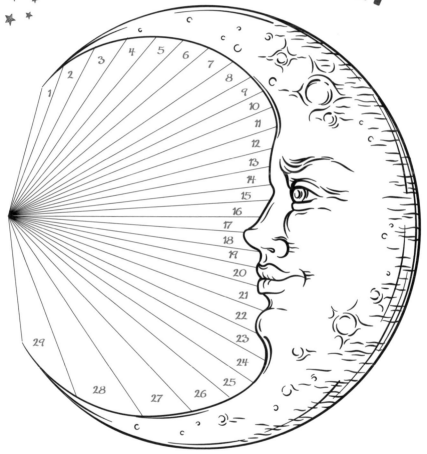

 Four hours or fewer

 Six hours

 Eight hours

Five hours

Seven hours

Nine hours or more

IT'S EASIER TO FEEL RELAXED

IN A SPACE THAT'S TIDY,

SO KEEP YOUR BEDROOM NEAT.

DECLUTTER IF YOU NEED TO,

OR ADD IN SOME EXTRA STORAGE

TO HELP YOU TO STAY ORGANIZED.

FOOD TRACKER

Very healthy

Mostly healthy

A little unhealthy

Very unhealthy

FRUIT AND VEGETABLE
TRACKER

1	11	21
2	12	22
3	13	23
4	14	24
5	15	25
6	16	26
7	17	27
8	18	28
9	19	29
10	20	

EACH PIECE = 1 OF YOUR 5 A DAY

ONE-DAY

Mood tracker

Date: _____

Pick any day of the month and colour in one section per hour
to get a snapshot of your mood over the course of a day.

☆ Great ☆ Good ☆ Average ☆ Poor ☆ Terrible

Positivity To-Do List:

Jot down a list of positive actions you can take this month,
ready to tick them off as you complete them.

☐ _____

☐ _____

☐ _____

☐ _____

☐ _____

☐ _____

☐ _____

☐ _____

☐ _____

☐ _____

Great Good Average Poor Terrible

HOW DO YOU FEEL?

Write down some of the words that describe how you're feeling.

ARE THERE FEELINGS YOU'D LIKE TO CHANGE?

Write down some actions to help you change the way you feel.

Comparing yourself to others will never make you feel good. Instead, compare yourself with yourself – and look how far you've come!

GLASS half FULL ?

Colour in how you felt this month on the glass below.

Fantastic

Great

Good

Average

Down

Bad

Terrible

Positivity
is
contagious

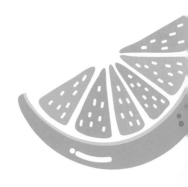

SLEEP TRACKER

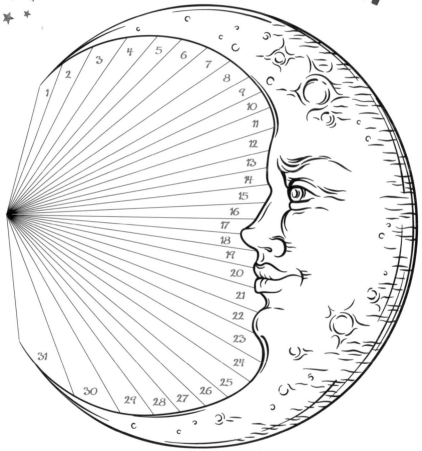

1 2 3 4 5 6 7 8 9 10 11 12 13 14 15 16 17 18 19 20 21 22 23 24 25 26 27 28 29 30 31

☐ Four hours or fewer

☐ Six hours

☐ Eight hours

☐ Five hours

☐ Seven hours

☐ Nine hours or more

WRITE IN A JOURNAL BEFORE
YOU GO TO SLEEP. GETTING
YOUR WORRIES OUT OF YOUR
HEAD AND ONTO PAPER CAN
HELP TO CLEAR YOUR MIND
AND MAKE YOU FEEL CALM.

FOOD TRACKER

Very healthy

A little unhealthy

Mostly healthy

Very unhealthy

EXERCISE
TRACKER

1 ♡♡♡♡♡	11 ♡♡♡♡♡	21 ♡♡♡♡♡
2 ♡♡♡♡♡	12 ♡♡♡♡♡	22 ♡♡♡♡♡
3 ♡♡♡♡♡	13 ♡♡♡♡♡	23 ♡♡♡♡♡
4 ♡♡♡♡♡	14 ♡♡♡♡♡	24 ♡♡♡♡♡
5 ♡♡♡♡♡	15 ♡♡♡♡♡	25 ♡♡♡♡♡
6 ♡♡♡♡♡	16 ♡♡♡♡♡	26 ♡♡♡♡♡
7 ♡♡♡♡♡	17 ♡♡♡♡♡	27 ♡♡♡♡♡
8 ♡♡♡♡♡	18 ♡♡♡♡♡	28 ♡♡♡♡♡
9 ♡♡♡♡♡	19 ♡♡♡♡♡	29 ♡♡♡♡♡
10 ♡♡♡♡♡	20 ♡♡♡♡♡	30 ♡♡♡♡♡
		31 ♡♡♡♡♡

EACH HEART = 6 MINS OF EXERCISE

ONE-DAY
Mood tracker

Date: _____

Pick any day of the month and colour in one section per hour
to get a snapshot of your mood over the course of a day.

☆ Great ☆ Good ☆ Average ☆ Poor ☆ Terrible

I promise to...

Use this page to note down a single promise that you will keep to improve your mood for the coming month. Revisit this page to remind yourself what you're committing to.

_____

_____

_____

_____

_____

_____

_____

_____

Great ♡ Good ♡ Average ♡ Poor ♡ Terrible

HOW DO YOU FEEL?

Write down some of the words that describe how you're feeling.

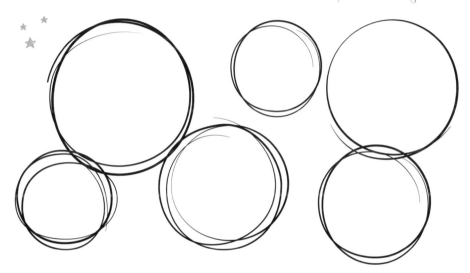

ARE THERE FEELINGS YOU'D LIKE TO CHANGE?

Write down some actions to help you change the way you feel.

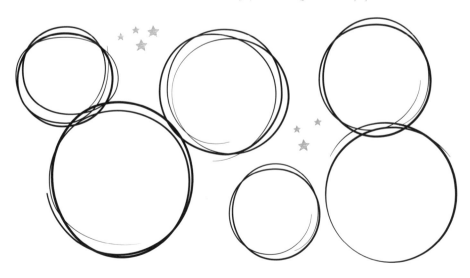

There's something good to be found in every day. Take a moment to think about three positive things that have happened, however small.

GLASS half FULL ?

Colour in how you felt this month on the glass below.

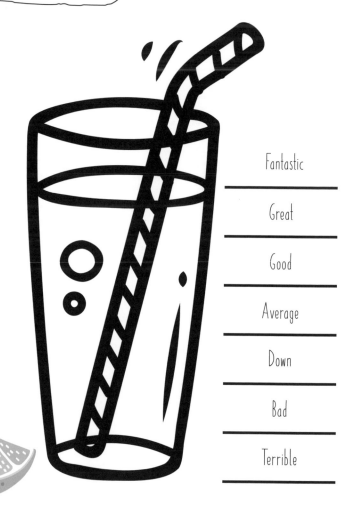

Fantastic

Great

Good

Average

Down

Bad

Terrible

MOUNTAINS ARE THERE TO BE CLIMBED

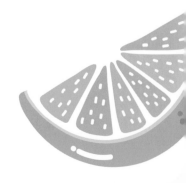

SLEEP TRACKER

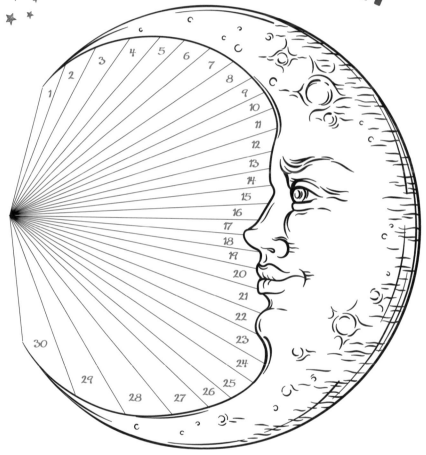

Four hours or fewer

Five hours

Six hours

Seven hours

Eight hours

Nine hours or more

DON'T USE YOUR BEDROOM
FOR WORKING, OR OTHER
ACTIVITIES DURING THE DAY.
TRY TO KEEP IT AS A SANCTUARY
— FOR SLEEP ONLY.

FOOD TRACKER

Very healthy

A little unhealthy

Mostly healthy

Very unhealthy

WATER

tracker

1 ◊◊◊◊◊	11 ◊◊◊◊◊	21 ◊◊◊◊◊
2 ◊◊◊◊◊	12 ◊◊◊◊◊	22 ◊◊◊◊◊
3 ◊◊◊◊◊	13 ◊◊◊◊◊	23 ◊◊◊◊◊
4 ◊◊◊◊◊	14 ◊◊◊◊◊	24 ◊◊◊◊◊
5 ◊◊◊◊◊	15 ◊◊◊◊◊	25 ◊◊◊◊◊
6 ◊◊◊◊◊	16 ◊◊◊◊◊	26 ◊◊◊◊◊
7 ◊◊◊◊◊	17 ◊◊◊◊◊	27 ◊◊◊◊◊
8 ◊◊◊◊◊	18 ◊◊◊◊◊	28 ◊◊◊◊◊
9 ◊◊◊◊◊	19 ◊◊◊◊◊	29 ◊◊◊◊◊
10 ◊◊◊◊◊	20 ◊◊◊◊◊	30 ◊◊◊◊◊

ONE DROP = 1 GLASS (400 ML)

ONE-DAY

Mood tracker

7
8
4 5
3 6
9
2
10
11
1
12

Date: _____

Pick any day of the month and colour in one section per hour
to get a snapshot of your mood over the course of a day.

Great   Good   Average   Poor   Terrible

Spring Playlist

Jot down your favourite energizing tunes that
will propel you through spring!

May

MOOD TRACKER

HOW DO YOU FEEL?

Write down some of the words that describe how you're feeling.

ARE THERE FEELINGS YOU'D LIKE TO CHANGE?

Write down some actions to help you change the way you feel.

Say no when you need
to. To feel your best,
it's important to give
yourself time and space,
and not to take on more
than you can handle.

GLASS half FULL ?

Colour in how you felt this month on the glass below.

Fantastic

Great

Good

Average

Down

Bad

Terrible

BE THE MASTER OF YOUR OWN DESTINY

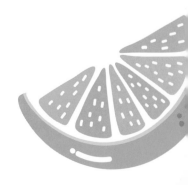

SLEEP TRACKER

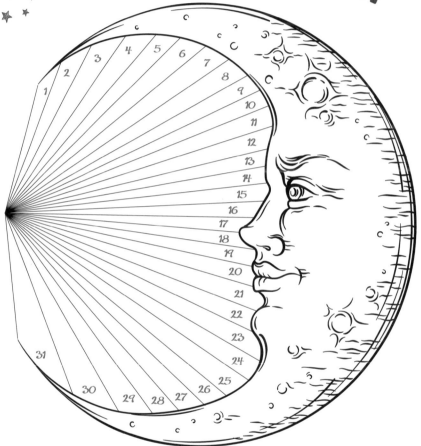

- ☐ Four hours or fewer
- ☐ Five hours
- ☐ Six hours
- ☐ Seven hours
- ☐ Eight hours
- ☐ Nine hours or more

ENJOY A HOT DRINK BEFORE
YOU GO TO BED, SUCH AS A
FRUIT TEA, DECAFFEINATED TEA
OR A CUP OF WARM MILK,
TO SOOTHE YOU INTO SLEEP.

FOOD TRACKER

Very healthy

A little unhealthy

Mostly healthy

Very unhealthy

FRUIT AND VEGETABLE
TRACKER

1 🍎🍎🍎🍎🍎   11 🍎🍎🍎🍎🍎   21 🍎🍎🍎🍎🍎

2 🍎🍎🍎🍎🍎   12 🍎🍎🍎🍎🍎   22 🍎🍎🍎🍎🍎

3 🍎🍎🍎🍎🍎   13 🍎🍎🍎🍎🍎   23 🍎🍎🍎🍎🍎

4 🍎🍎🍎🍎🍎   14 🍎🍎🍎🍎🍎   24 🍎🍎🍎🍎🍎

5 🍎🍎🍎🍎🍎   15 🍎🍎🍎🍎🍎   25 🍎🍎🍎🍎🍎

6 🍎🍎🍎🍎🍎   16 🍎🍎🍎🍎🍎   26 🍎🍎🍎🍎🍎

7 🍎🍎🍎🍎🍎   17 🍎🍎🍎🍎🍎   27 🍎🍎🍎🍎🍎

8 🍎🍎🍎🍎🍎   18 🍎🍎🍎🍎🍎   28 🍎🍎🍎🍎🍎

9 🍎🍎🍎🍎🍎   19 🍎🍎🍎🍎🍎   29 🍎🍎🍎🍎🍎

10 🍎🍎🍎🍎🍎   20 🍎🍎🍎🍎🍎   30 🍎🍎🍎🍎🍎

EACH PIECE = 1 OF YOUR 5 A DAY   31 🍎🍎🍎🍎🍎

ONE-DAY

Mood tracker

Date: _____

Pick any day of the month and colour in one section per hour
to get a snapshot of your mood over the course of a day.

Great · Good · Average · Poor · Terrible

GRATITUDE LIST:

Think about ten things in life that you are grateful for right
now - even the smallest things - and make a list of them here.
Every time you need a pick-me-up, reflect back on this list.

- [ ] _____
- [ ] _____
- [ ] _____
- [ ] _____
- [ ] _____
- [ ] _____
- [ ] _____
- [ ] _____
- [ ] _____
- [ ] _____

JUNE

MOOD TRACKER

HOW DO YOU FEEL?

Write down some of the words that describe how you're feeling.

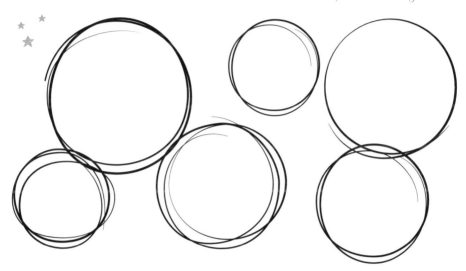

ARE THERE FEELINGS YOU'D LIKE TO CHANGE?

Write down some actions to help you change the way you feel.

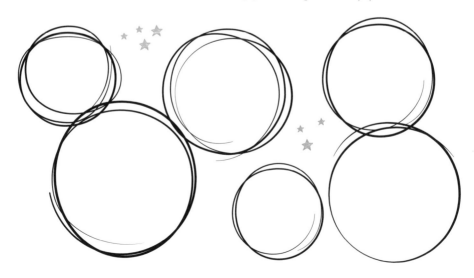

Try to make time every

day to get some fresh air.

Even a ten-minute walk

can blow away the cobwebs

and leave you feeling

bright and refreshed.

GLASS half FULL ?

Colour in how you felt this month on the glass below.

Fantastic

Great

Good

Average

Down

Bad

Terrible

WINDING
PATHS LEAD
TO THE MOST
INTERESTING
PLACES

SLEEP TRACKER

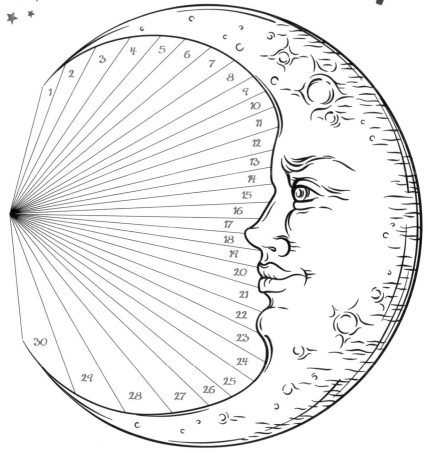

☐	Four hours or fewer	☐ Six hours	☐ Eight hours
☐	Five hours	☐ Seven hours	☐ Nine hours or more

SIT ANYWHERE YOU FEEL
COMFORTABLE AND CLOSE YOUR
EYES. BREATHE IN SLOWLY THROUGH
YOUR NOSE UNTIL YOUR LUNGS ARE
FULL. HOLD FOR FOUR LONG COUNTS,
THEN EXHALE SLOWLY. REPEAT
UNTIL YOU ARE FEELING CALM.

FOOD TRACKER

Very healthy

A little unhealthy

Mostly healthy

Very unhealthy

EXERCISE TRACKER

1 ♡♡♡♡♡	11 ♡♡♡♡♡	21 ♡♡♡♡♡
2 ♡♡♡♡♡	12 ♡♡♡♡♡	22 ♡♡♡♡♡
3 ♡♡♡♡♡	13 ♡♡♡♡♡	23 ♡♡♡♡♡
4 ♡♡♡♡♡	14 ♡♡♡♡♡	24 ♡♡♡♡♡
5 ♡♡♡♡♡	15 ♡♡♡♡♡	25 ♡♡♡♡♡
6 ♡♡♡♡♡	16 ♡♡♡♡♡	26 ♡♡♡♡♡
7 ♡♡♡♡♡	17 ♡♡♡♡♡	27 ♡♡♡♡♡
8 ♡♡♡♡♡	18 ♡♡♡♡♡	28 ♡♡♡♡♡
9 ♡♡♡♡♡	19 ♡♡♡♡♡	29 ♡♡♡♡♡
10 ♡♡♡♡♡	20 ♡♡♡♡♡	30 ♡♡♡♡♡

EACH HEART = 6 MINS OF EXERCISE

ONE-DAY
Mood tracker

Pick any day of the month and colour in one section per hour to get a snapshot of your mood over the course of a day.

Date: _____

 Great Good Average Poor Terrible

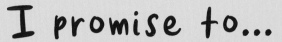

I promise to...

Use this page to note down a single promise that you will keep to improve your mood for the coming month. Revisit this page to remind yourself what you're committing to.

_____

_____

_____

_____

_____

_____

_____

_____

July
MOOD TRACKER

HOW DO YOU FEEL?

Write down some of the words that describe how you're feeling.

ARE THERE FEELINGS YOU'D LIKE TO CHANGE?

Write down some actions to help you change the way you feel.

Life is full of little problems and everyday annoyances – but holding onto them all is exhausting! Just let them go, and allow yourself to be calm.

GLASS half FULL ?

Colour in how you felt this month on the glass below.

Fantastic

Great

Good

Average

Down

Bad

Terrible

IF YOUR DREAMS RUN, CHASE THEM

SLEEP TRACKER

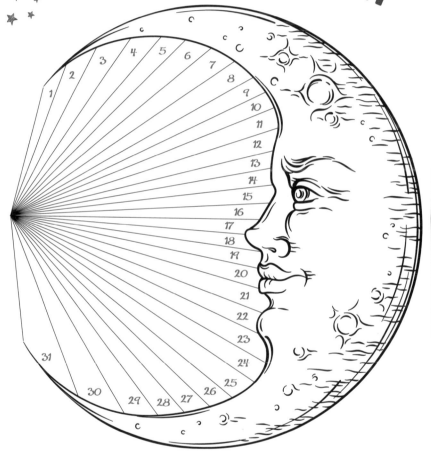

 Four hours or fewer

 Six hours

 Eight hours

Five hours

Seven hours

Nine hours or more

FOR A BETTER NIGHT'S SLEEP,
STAY COOL. OPEN A WINDOW
OR DOOR, WEAR BREATHABLE
PYJAMAS, OR OPT FOR LIGHTWEIGHT
BEDDING TO HELP YOU STAY
COMFORTABLE DURING THE NIGHT.

FOOD TRACKER

☐ Very healthy   ☐ A little unhealthy

☐ Mostly healthy   ☐ Very unhealthy

WATER

tracker

1 ⟁⟁⟁⟁⟁	11 ⟁⟁⟁⟁⟁	21 ⟁⟁⟁⟁⟁
2 ⟁⟁⟁⟁⟁	12 ⟁⟁⟁⟁⟁	22 ⟁⟁⟁⟁⟁
3 ⟁⟁⟁⟁⟁	13 ⟁⟁⟁⟁⟁	23 ⟁⟁⟁⟁⟁
4 ⟁⟁⟁⟁⟁	14 ⟁⟁⟁⟁⟁	24 ⟁⟁⟁⟁⟁
5 ⟁⟁⟁⟁⟁	15 ⟁⟁⟁⟁⟁	25 ⟁⟁⟁⟁⟁
6 ⟁⟁⟁⟁⟁	16 ⟁⟁⟁⟁⟁	26 ⟁⟁⟁⟁⟁
7 ⟁⟁⟁⟁⟁	17 ⟁⟁⟁⟁⟁	27 ⟁⟁⟁⟁⟁
8 ⟁⟁⟁⟁⟁	18 ⟁⟁⟁⟁⟁	28 ⟁⟁⟁⟁⟁
9 ⟁⟁⟁⟁⟁	19 ⟁⟁⟁⟁⟁	29 ⟁⟁⟁⟁⟁
10 ⟁⟁⟁⟁⟁	20 ⟁⟁⟁⟁⟁	30 ⟁⟁⟁⟁⟁

ONE DROP = I GLASS (400 ML)   31 ⟁⟁⟁⟁⟁

ONE-DAY
Mood tracker

Date: _____

Pick any day of the month and colour in one section per hour
to get a snapshot of your mood over the course of a day.

☆ Great ☆ Good ☆ Average ☆ Poor ☆ Terrible

Summer Playlist

Make a playlist of your favourite sounds for when
you need to dance like no one is watching!

1. _____
2. _____
3. _____
4. _____
5. _____
6. _____
7. _____
8. _____
9. _____
10. _____

august

MOOD TRACKER

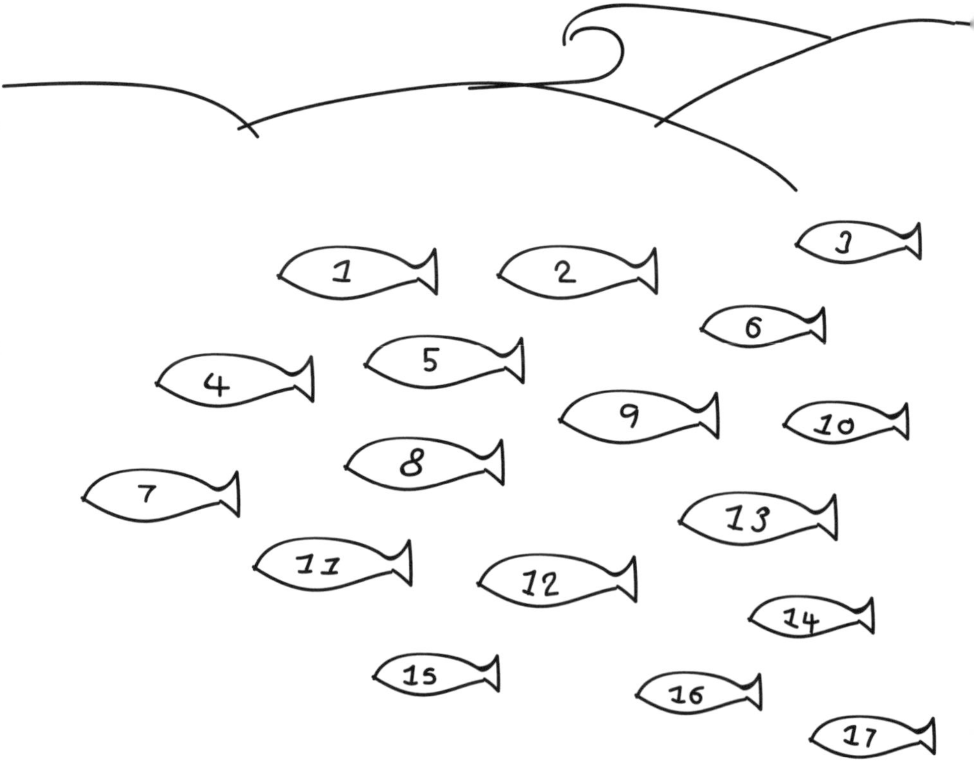

1
2
3
4
5
6
7
8
9
10
11
12
13
14
15
16
17

18 19 20 21 22 23 24 25 26 27 28 29 30 31

Great Good Average Poor Terrible

HOW DO YOU FEEL?

Write down some of the words that describe how you're feeling.

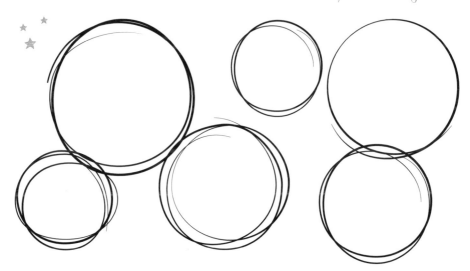

ARE THERE FEELINGS YOU'D LIKE TO CHANGE?

Write down some actions to help you change the way you feel.

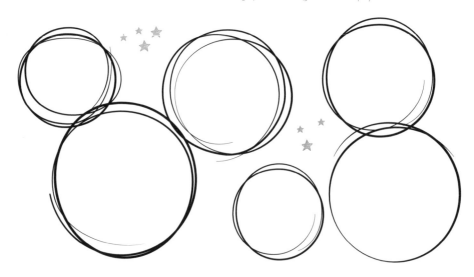

Note to self

Any goal worth
achieving usually
takes perseverance
and hard work, so
don't be disheartened
by obstacles.

GLASS half FULL ?

Colour in how you felt this
month on the glass below.

Fantastic

Great

Good

Average

Down

Bad

Terrible

YOUR LIFE IS A BOOK — MAKE EVERY CHAPTER COUNT

SLEEP TRACKER

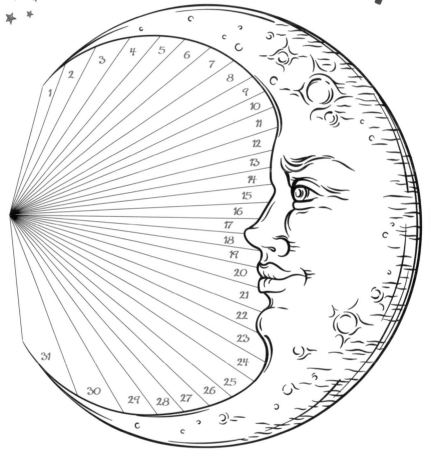

1 2 3 4 5 6 7 8 9 10 11 12 13 14 15 16 17 18 19 20 21 22 23 24 25 26 27 28 29 30 31

☐ Four hours or fewer

☐ Five hours

☐ Six hours

☐ Seven hours

☐ Eight hours

☐ Nine hours or more

HAVE GENTLE LIGHTING
IN YOUR BEDROOM TO HELP
EASE THE TRANSITION FROM DAY
TO NIGHT. THE LOWER LIGHT WILL
HELP SIGNAL TO YOUR BODY
THAT IT'S TIME TO SLEEP.

FOOD TRACKER

30 31 1 2 3 4 5 6 7 8 9 10 11 12 13 14 15 16 17 18 19 20 21 22 23 24 25 26 27 28 29

☐ Very healthy   ☐ A little unhealthy

☐ Mostly healthy   ☐ Very unhealthy

FRUIT AND VEGETABLE
TRACKER

1	11	21
2	12	22
3	13	23
4	14	24
5	15	25
6	16	26
7	17	27
8	18	28
9	19	29
10	20	30
		31

EACH PIECE = 1 OF YOUR 5 A DAY

ONE-DAY

Mood tracker

9

10

7

6

11

5

8

4

12

3

2

1

Pick any day of the month and colour in one section per hour
to get a snapshot of your mood over the course of a day.

☆ Great ☆ Good ☆ Average ☆ Poor ☆ Terrible

"Shake Things Up" List:

It's easy to get stuck in a rut and go about your life on autopilot. Jot down a list of small changes you could make to your everyday routine to shake things up – such as doing ten minutes of yoga in the mornings, having something different for lunch, or calling a friend in the evening. Tick them off as you complete them.

☐ _____

☐ _____

☐ _____

☐ _____

☐ _____

☐ _____

☐ _____

☐ _____

☐ _____

☐ _____

September

MOOD TRACKER

HOW DO YOU FEEL?

Write down some of the words that describe how you're feeling.

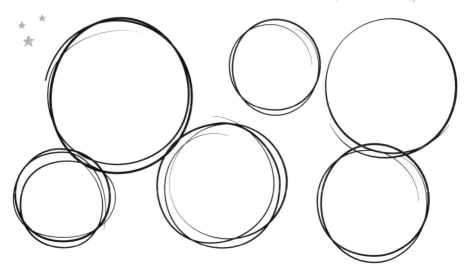

ARE THERE FEELINGS YOU'D LIKE TO CHANGE?

Write down some actions to help you change the way you feel.

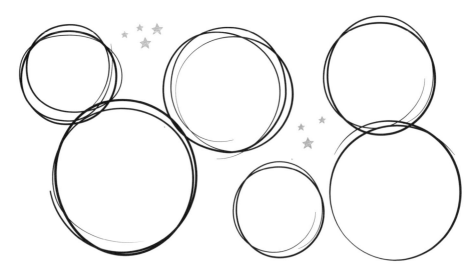

Take a moment to pause
every day. It's easy to
forget amid our busy
lives, but five minutes
of calm and quiet can
make a huge difference
to how you feel.

GLASS half FULL?

Colour in how you felt this month on the glass below.

Fantastic

Great

Good

Average

Down

Bad

Terrible

TRUST IN YOURSELF

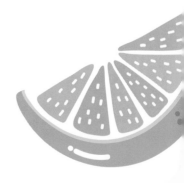

SLEEP TRACKER

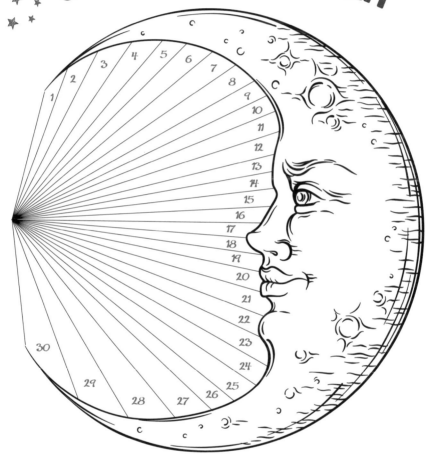

Four hours or fewer

Five hours

Six hours

Seven hours

Eight hours

Nine hours or more

MAKE YOUR BEDROOM AS DARK
AS POSSIBLE TO HELP YOU FALL
AND STAY ASLEEP. BLOCK OUT
THE LIGHT WITH HEAVY CURTAINS,
OR CONSIDER USING AN EYE MASK.

FOOD TRACKER

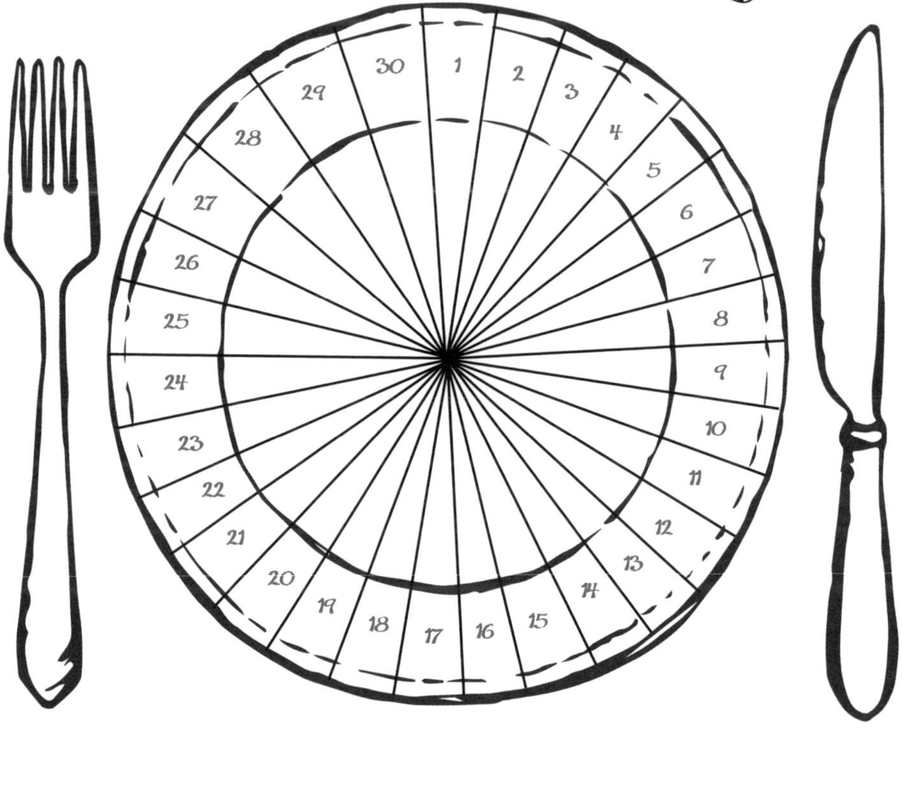

- ☐ Very healthy
- ☐ A little unhealthy
- ☐ Mostly healthy
- ☐ Very unhealthy

EXERCISE
TRACKER

1 ♡♡♡♡♡	11 ♡♡♡♡♡	21 ♡♡♡♡♡
2 ♡♡♡♡♡	12 ♡♡♡♡♡	22 ♡♡♡♡♡
3 ♡♡♡♡♡	13 ♡♡♡♡♡	23 ♡♡♡♡♡
4 ♡♡♡♡♡	14 ♡♡♡♡♡	24 ♡♡♡♡♡
5 ♡♡♡♡♡	15 ♡♡♡♡♡	25 ♡♡♡♡♡
6 ♡♡♡♡♡	16 ♡♡♡♡♡	26 ♡♡♡♡♡
7 ♡♡♡♡♡	17 ♡♡♡♡♡	27 ♡♡♡♡♡
8 ♡♡♡♡♡	18 ♡♡♡♡♡	28 ♡♡♡♡♡
9 ♡♡♡♡♡	19 ♡♡♡♡♡	29 ♡♡♡♡♡
10 ♡♡♡♡♡	20 ♡♡♡♡♡	30 ♡♡♡♡♡

EACH HEART = 6 MINS OF EXERCISE

ONE-DAY
Mood tracker

Date: _____

Pick any day of the month and colour in one section per hour to get a snapshot of your mood over the course of a day.

☆ Great   ☆ Good   ☆ Average   ☆ Poor   ☆ Terrible

I promise to...

Use this page to note down a single promise that you will keep to improve your mood over the coming month. Revisit this page to remind yourself what you're committing to.

_____

_____

_____

_____

_____

_____

_____

_____

_____

HOW DO YOU FEEL?

Write down some of the words that describe how you're feeling.

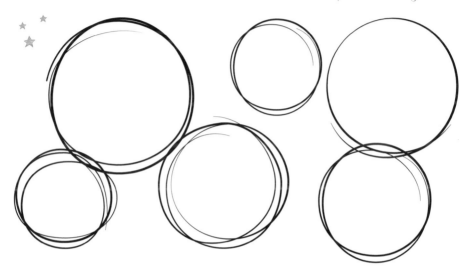

ARE THERE FEELINGS YOU'D LIKE TO CHANGE?

Write down some actions to help you change the way you feel.

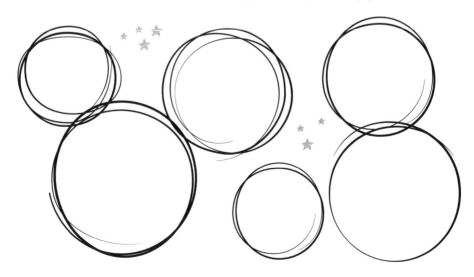

Surround yourself

with positive people

who support you and

make you feel good.

GLaSS half FULL ?

Colour in how you felt this month on the glass below.

Fantastic
_____

Great
_____

Good
_____

Average
_____

Down
_____

Bad
_____

Terrible
_____

RISE
TO THE
CHALLENGE

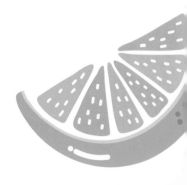

SLEEP TRACKER

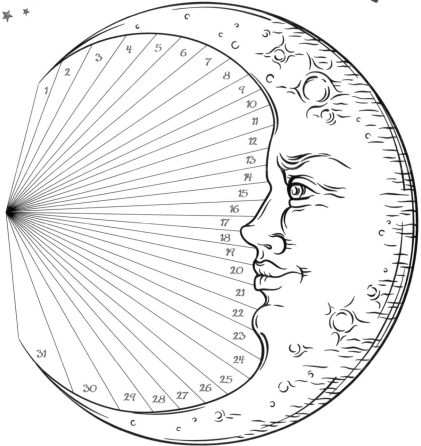

☐ Four hours or fewer   ☐ Six hours   ☐ Eight hours

☐ Five hours   ☐ Seven hours   ☐ Nine hours or more

EXERCISE DURING THE DAY FOR A
BETTER NIGHT'S SLEEP. AS WELL
AS KEEPING YOUR BODY HEALTHY,
EXERCISE HELPS TO KEEP THE
BRAIN'S NEUROTRANSMITTERS IN
BALANCE — WHICH, IN TURN,
HELPS YOU TO SLEEP BETTER.

FOOD TRACKER

| Very healthy | | A little unhealthy |
| Mostly healthy | | Very unhealthy |

WATER
tracker

1 ⬦⬦⬦⬦⬦	11 ⬦⬦⬦⬦⬦	21 ⬦⬦⬦⬦⬦
2 ⬦⬦⬦⬦⬦	12 ⬦⬦⬦⬦⬦	22 ⬦⬦⬦⬦⬦
3 ⬦⬦⬦⬦⬦	13 ⬦⬦⬦⬦⬦	23 ⬦⬦⬦⬦⬦
4 ⬦⬦⬦⬦⬦	14 ⬦⬦⬦⬦⬦	24 ⬦⬦⬦⬦⬦
5 ⬦⬦⬦⬦⬦	15 ⬦⬦⬦⬦⬦	25 ⬦⬦⬦⬦⬦
6 ⬦⬦⬦⬦⬦	16 ⬦⬦⬦⬦⬦	26 ⬦⬦⬦⬦⬦
7 ⬦⬦⬦⬦⬦	17 ⬦⬦⬦⬦⬦	27 ⬦⬦⬦⬦⬦
8 ⬦⬦⬦⬦⬦	18 ⬦⬦⬦⬦⬦	28 ⬦⬦⬦⬦⬦
9 ⬦⬦⬦⬦⬦	19 ⬦⬦⬦⬦⬦	29 ⬦⬦⬦⬦⬦
10 ⬦⬦⬦⬦⬦	20 ⬦⬦⬦⬦⬦	30 ⬦⬦⬦⬦⬦

ONE DROP = 1 GLASS (400 ML)   31 ⬦⬦⬦⬦⬦

ONE-DAY

Mood tracker

Date: _____

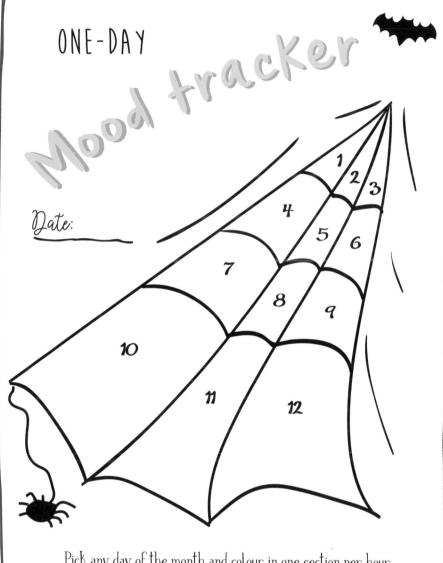

Pick any day of the month and colour in one section per hour
to get a snapshot of your mood over the course of a day.

☆ Great ☆ Good ☆ Average ☆ Poor ☆ Terrible

Autumn Playlist

Jot down the tunes that will get you cosy this autumn.

1. _____
2. _____
3. _____
4. _____
5. _____
6. _____
7. _____
8. _____
9. _____
10. _____

NOVEMBER
MOOD TRACKER

Great ⭐ Good ⭐ Average ⭐ Poor ⭐ Terrible

HOW DO YOU FEEL?

Write down some of the words that describe how you're feeling.

ARE THERE FEELINGS YOU'D LIKE TO CHANGE?

Write down some actions to help you change the way you feel.

Don't be afraid to ask for help. We can't go through life alone, so reach out for support when you need it.

GLASS half FULL?

Colour in how you felt this month on the glass below.

Fantastic

Great

Good

Average

Down

Bad

Terrible

SHOW THE WORLD WHAT YOU'RE MADE OF!

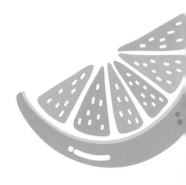

SLEEP TRACKER

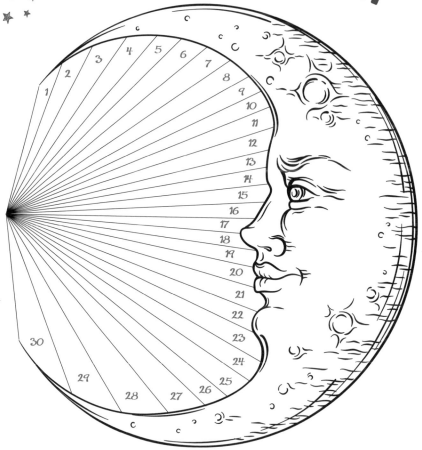

☐ Four hours or fewer

☐ Five hours

☐ Six hours

☐ Seven hours

☐ Eight hours

☐ Nine hours or more

SWITCH OFF YOUR GADGETS
AT LEAST HALF AN HOUR
BEFORE BEDTIME TO ALLOW
YOUR MIND TO WIND DOWN
AND PREPARE ITSELF FOR SLEEP.

FOOD TRACKER

 Very healthy

 A little unhealthy

 Mostly healthy

 Very unhealthy

FRUIT AND VEGETABLE
TRACKER

1	11	21
2	12	22
3	13	23
4	14	24
5	15	25
6	16	26
7	17	27
8	18	28
9	19	29
10	20	30

EACH PIECE = 1 OF YOUR 5 A DAY

ONE-DAY
Mood tracker

1
12
2
3
4
5
6
7
8
9
11
10

Date: _____

Pick any day of the month and colour in one section per hour
to get a snapshot of your mood over the course of a day.

☆ Great ☆ Good ☆ Average ☆ Poor ☆ Terrible

Positivity To-Do List:

Think about ten things in life that you are grateful for right now - even the smallest things - and make a list of them here. Every time you need a pick-me-up reflect back on this list.

- [ ] _____
- [ ] _____
- [ ] _____
- [ ] _____
- [ ] _____
- [ ] _____
- [ ] _____
- [ ] _____
- [ ] _____
- [ ] _____

December

MOOD TRACKER

17 18 19 20 21

22 23 24 25 26

27 28 29 30 31

Great Good Average Poor Terrible

HOW DO YOU FEEL?

Write down some of the words that describe how you're feeling.

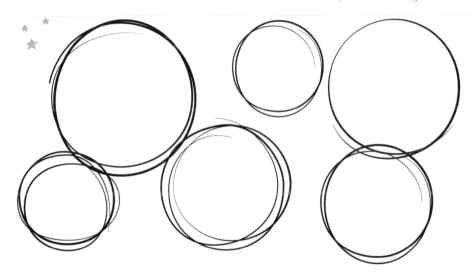

ARE THERE FEELINGS YOU'D LIKE TO CHANGE?

Write down some actions to help you change the way you feel.

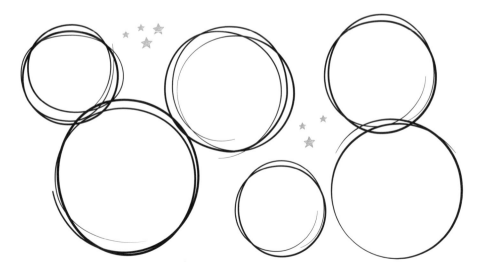

Note to self

Believe in yourself and others will believe in you too. Approach life with your head held high and let your inner light shine out.

GLASS half FULL?

Colour in how you felt this month on the glass below.

Fantastic

Great

Good

Average

Down

Bad

Terrible

IF AN OPPORTUNITY ARISES, DON'T HESITATE

SLEEP TRACKER

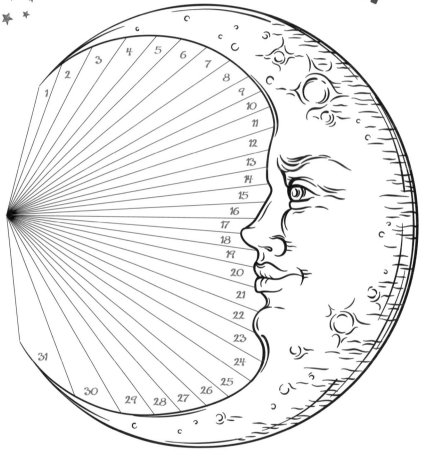

 Four hours or fewer

Six hours

Eight hours

Five hours

 Seven hours

 Nine hours or more

HAVE A BEDTIME ROUTINE.
TRY TO GO TO BED AT ROUGHLY
THE SAME TIME EVERY DAY
SO THAT, WHEN YOU LIE DOWN
AND CLOSE YOUR EYES, YOUR
BODY IS EXPECTING TO SLEEP.

FOOD
TRACKER

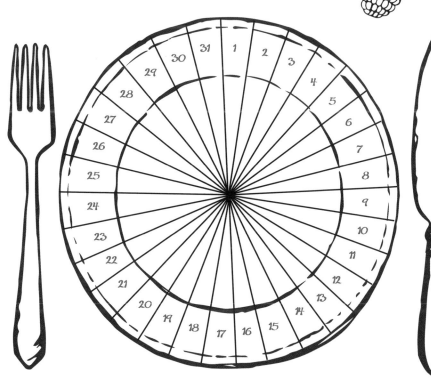

30 31 1 2
29 3
28 4
27 5
26 6
25 7
24 8
23 9
22 10
21 11
20 12
19 13
18 14
17 16 15

☐ Very healthy   ☐ A little unhealthy

☐ Mostly healthy   ☐ Very unhealthy

EXERCISE TRACKER

1 ♡♡♡♡♡	11 ♡♡♡♡♡	21 ♡♡♡♡♡
2 ♡♡♡♡♡	12 ♡♡♡♡♡	22 ♡♡♡♡♡
3 ♡♡♡♡♡	13 ♡♡♡♡♡	23 ♡♡♡♡♡
4 ♡♡♡♡♡	14 ♡♡♡♡♡	24 ♡♡♡♡♡
5 ♡♡♡♡♡	15 ♡♡♡♡♡	25 ♡♡♡♡♡
6 ♡♡♡♡♡	16 ♡♡♡♡♡	26 ♡♡♡♡♡
7 ♡♡♡♡♡	17 ♡♡♡♡♡	27 ♡♡♡♡♡
8 ♡♡♡♡♡	18 ♡♡♡♡♡	28 ♡♡♡♡♡
9 ♡♡♡♡♡	19 ♡♡♡♡♡	29 ♡♡♡♡♡
10 ♡♡♡♡♡	20 ♡♡♡♡♡	30 ♡♡♡♡♡
		31 ♡♡♡♡♡

EACH HEART = 6 MINS OF EXERCISE

ONE-DAY Mood tracker

1
2
3
4
5
6
7
8
9
10
11
12

Date: ____________

Pick any day of the month and colour in one section per hour to get a snapshot of your mood over the course of a day.

Great
Good
Average
Poor
Terrible

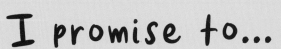

I promise to...

Use this page to note down a single promise that you will keep to improve your mood over the coming month. Revisit this page to remind yourself what you're committing to.

_____

_____

_____

_____

_____

_____

_____

_____

CONGRATULATIONS — YOU'VE TRACKED YOURSELF FOR A WHOLE YEAR!

Now that you've reached the end of this book, take a look back over the last twelve months to see your journey. What does it show you? What have you learned? How do you want to continue?

Even a few minutes a day spent taking note of how you feel can help you to be more present and more in tune with yourself. We hope that this book has given you space to reflect and provided you with insight, so that you can now continue your journey with a better understanding of how you and your mind work together.

Notes

Notes

Notes

Notes

Notes

Notes

Notes

If you're interested in finding out more about our books, find us on Facebook at Summersdale Publishers, follow us on Twitter at @Summersdale and follow our Instagram @summersdalepublishers.

Thanks very much for buying this Summersdale book.

www.summersdale.com